U AR-E

D1562574

S*PeRM**K*T

Acknowledgments

My heartfelt thanks to Nathaniel Mackey of *Hambone*, Mark Nowak of *Furnitures*, and Jessica Grim and Melanie Neilson of *Big Allis*, who first published parts of *S*PeRM**K*T*.

Publication of this book was made possible, in part, by a grant from the Commonwealth of Pennsylvania Council on the Arts.

Book design by Gil Ott.
Singing Horse Press
PO Box 40034
Philadelphia   PA   19106
(215) 844-7678

ISBN: 0-935162-12-7

S*PeRM**K*T

Harryette Mullen

Singing Horse Press

Lines assemble gutter and margin. Outside and in, they straighten a place. Organize a stand. Shelve space. Square footage. Align your list or listlessness. Pushing oddly evening aisle catches the tail of an eye. Displays the cherished share. Individually wrapped singles, frozen divorced compartments, six-pack widows express themselves while women wait in family ways, all bulging baskets, squirming young. More on line incites the eyes. Bold names label familiar type faces. Her hand scanning throwaway lines.

With eternal welcome mats omniscient doors swing open offering temptation, redemption, thrilling confessions. The state of Grace is Monaco. A shrine in Memphis, colossal savings. A single serving after-work lives. In sanctuaries of the sublime subliminal mobius soundtrack backs spatial mnemonics, radiant stations of the crass. When you see it, you remember what you came for.

Pyramids are eroding monuments. Embalmed soup stocks the recyclable soul adrift in its newspaper boat of double coupons. Seconds decline in descent from number one, top of the heap. So this is generic life, feeding from a dented cant. Devoid of colored labels, the discounted irregulars.

Just add water. That homespun incantation activates potent powders, alchemical concentrates, jars and boxes of abracadabra. Bottled water works trickling down a rainy day watering can reconstitute the shrinking dollar. A greenback garnered from a tree. At two bucks, one tender legal portrait of Saint No-Nicks stands in for clean-shaven, defunct cherry chopper. Check out this week's seasonal electric reindeer *luz de vela* Virgin Mary mark downs. Choose from ten brands clearly miracle H-2-O. Pure genius in a bottle. Not municipal precipitate you pay to tap, but dear rain fresh capped at spring. Cleaner than North Pole snow, or Commander in Chief's hard-boiled white collars. Purer than pale saint's flow of holy beard or drops distilled from sterile virgin tears.

Aren't you glad you use petroleum? Don't wait to be told you explode. You're not fully here until you're over there. Never let them see you eat. You might be taken for a zoo. Raise your hand if you're sure you're not.

Desperately pregnant nubile preferred stock girls deliver perfect healthy psychic space alien test tube babes, in ten or less, or yours is free, we guarantee.

It must be white, a picture of health, the spongy napkin made to blot blood. Dainty paper soaks up leaks that steaks splayed on trays are oozing. Lights replace the blush red flesh is losing. Cutlets leak. Tenderloins bleed pink light. Plastic wrap bandages marbled slabs in sanitary packaging made to be stained. A three-hanky picture of feminine hygiene.

Iron maidens make docile martyrs. Their bodies on the racks stretched taut. Honing hunger to perfect, aglow in nimbus flash. A few lean slicks, to cover a multitude, fix a feast for the eyes. They starve for all the things we crave.

Chill out a cold, cold world. Open frost-free fridget. Thaw and serve slightly deferred gratification, plucked from the frozone, hard packed as slab of ice aged mammoth. Cool cache stashed between carbon dated ziplocked leftovers and soothing multicolored safety tested plastic teething ring.

Kills bugs dead. Redundancy is syntactical overkill. A pinprick of peace at the end of the tunnel of a nightmare night in a roach motel. Their noise infects the dream. In black kitchens they foul the food, walk on our bodies as we sleep over oceans of pirate flags. Skull and crossbones, they crunch like candy. When we die they will eat us, unless we kill them first. Invest in better mousetraps. Take no prisoners on board ship, to rock the boat, to violate our beds with pestilence. We dream the dream of extirpation. Wipe out a species, with God on our side. Annihilate the insects. Sterilize the filthy vermin.

A daughter turned against the grain refuses your gleanings, denies your milk, soggy absorbency she abhors. Chokes on your words when asked about love. Never would swallow the husks you're allowed. Not a spoonful gets down what you see of her now. Crisp image from disciplined form. Torn hostage ripening out of hand. Boxtop trophy of war, brings to the table a regimen from hell. At breakfast shuts out all nurturant murmurs. Holds against you the eating for two. Why brag of pain a body can't remember? You pretend once again she's not lost forever.

Nine out of ten docks trash paper or plastic. My shrink wraps securely stashed and shredded freshness re-enforced double baggage. All tidy toxic clean dregs folded down in dumps with safety improved twist-off tops. Crumpled sheets, sweating ammunition. A strychnine migraine is a p.r. problem. Every orifice leaks. No cap is tamper proof.

Chow down on all floors. Nuzzle shallow dishes. Swallow spittle lapping muzzles. Doggie style fashions better leather collars. Caressed pets milk bone bandits. Checkerboard square, clean as houndstooth. Rub a rawhide bone up out back. See Rover choose a rubber toy over puppy kibble. Poodle grooming lather bothers a tick. A bomb goes off to rid a house of pests. Yet pets are loyal and true watch dogs take a licking while nestling birds feather bed and beak fast kisses. Cat nips flannel mouse. Kitty litters kittens.

Plushy soft tissues off screen generic rolls as the world turns on re-vivid revival rewinds reruns recycling itself. A box of blue movie equals smurf sex. Poor peewee couldn't shake it. Wished he had a bigger one. Per inch of clear resolution's color window, more thick squares snag a softer touch.

Two thousand flushes drain her white porcelana, chlorinsed with antistepton disinfunktant unknownabrasives, cleanliness gets next to.

In specks finds nothing amiss. Rubs a glove on lemony wood. But the gleam of a sigh at a spotless rinsed dish. Spots herself in its service, buffed and rebuffed. Shines on the gloss of birds eye drop leaf maple tabletop. Pledges a new leaf shining her future polishing skills. The silver dropped at dinner announces the arrival of a woman at a fork. She beams at a waxing moon.

What's brewing when a guy pops the top off a bottle or can talk with another man after a real good sweat. It opens, pours a cold stream of the great outdoors. Hunting a wild six-pack reminds him of football and women and other blood spoors. Frequent channels keep high volume foamy liquids overflowing, not to be contained. Champs, heroes, hard workers all back-lit with ornate gold of cowboy sunset lift dashing white heads, those burly mugs.

Off the pig, ya dig? He squeals, grease the sucker. Hack that fatback, pour the pork. Pig out, rib the fellas. Ham it up, hype the tripe. Save your bacon, bring home some. Sweet dreams pigmeat. Pork belly futures, larded accounts, hog heaven. Little piggish to market. Tub of guts hog wilding. A pig of yourself, high on swine, cries all the way home. Streak a lean gets away cleaner than Safeway chitlings. That's all, folks.

Well bread ain't refined of coarse dark textures never enriched a doughty peasant. The rich finely powdered with soft white flours. Then poor got pasty pale and pure blands ingrained inbred. Roll out dough we need so what bread fortifies their minimum daily sandwich. Here's a dry wry toast for a rough age when darker richer upper crust, flourishing, outpriced the staff with moral fiber. Brown and serve, a slice of life whose side's your butter on.

A dream of eggplant or zucchini may produce fresh desires. Some fruits are vegetables. The way we bruise and wilt, all perishable.

Bad germs get zapped by secret agents in formulaic new improved scientific solutions. Ivory says pure nuff and snowflakes be white enough to do the dirty work. Step and fetch laundry tumbles out shuffling into sorted colored stacks. That black grape of underwear fame denies paternity of claymate raisinets. Swinging burgers do a soft shoe, gringo derbies tipping latina banana. Some giggling lump of dough, an infantile chef, smiles animatedly at his fresh little sis. They never gits a tan in the heartwarming easy bake oven because they is eternal raw ingredients for programmed microwavering halfbaked expressions of family love.

Toejam must cause jelly don't. Mink chocolate melts in you.

Champagne dreams wet shammy softy. Hands-on carwash, a pampering. Bathtub's a cheap vacation. Cruising her archipelago, laid back with turn-on pages. Emerged from placid stacked suds, hyperbolic exotic aisle of glamour bubbles. Pearl diver's paradise. All sparkling steel and spritzed crystal rubbed down clean to the squeak. A body with an interior rolls out sleek waxed shiny hard enameled. It takes her away, that seductive new smell, in fourteen flavors. She's cherry, just driving off the lot.

Eat junk, don't shoot. Fast food leaves hunger off the hook. Employees must wash hands. Bleach your needles, cook the works. Stick it to the frying pan, hyped again. Another teflon prez. Caught in the fire 'round midnight, quick and dirty biz. Smoked in the self-cleaning oven.

How anorexics treat themselves. Sucking slim mint for the breathless, rationed yet tingling indulgence. Over-counters prescribe themselves slighter than any other lifetime of fractioned unburned energy hands down all ads up. How fresh in your mouth to eat a sweet thought minus the need to work off guilt, to amortize the cost.

Slow ketchup, slower. Dark coffee, darker. Nice white rice. Meat is real. Clean meat. Trimmed, not bloody.

Past perfect food sticks in the craw. Curdles the pulse. Coops up otherwise free ranging birds whose plucked wings beat hearts over easy. Flapping aerobically, cocks walk on brittle zeros. They make and break and scramble to get ahead. Whisk the yokels into shape. Use their pecker order to separate the whites.

Seeds in packets brighter than soup cans, cheaper than lottery tickets, more hopeful than waxed rutabagas, promising order in alphabetized envelopes, dream startled gardens one spring day tore open. Sown in good dirt, fingered tenderly.

Ad infinitum perpetual infants goo. Pastel puree of pure pink bland blue-eyed babes all born a cute blond with no chronic colic. Sterile eugenically cloned rows of clean rosy dimples and pamper proof towhead cowlicks. Adorable babyface jars. Sturdy innocent in the pink, out of the blue packs disposing durable superabsorbent miracle fibers. As solids break down, go to waste, a land fills up dead diapers with funky halflife.

Refreshing spearmint gums up the words. Instant permkit combs through the wreckage. Bigger better spermkit grins down family of four. Scratch and sniff your lucky number. You may already be a wiener.

Hide the face. Chase dirt with an ugly stick. That sinking sensation, a sponge dive. Brush off scum on some well scrubbed mission. It's slick to admit, motherwit and grit ain't groceries.

Flies in buttermilk. What a fellowship. That's why white milk makes yellow butter. Homo means the same. A woman is different. Cream always rises over split milk. Muscle men drink it all in. Awesome teeth and wholesale bones. Our cows are well adjusted. The lost family album keeps saying cheese. Speed readers skim the white space of this galaxy.

R BRAND LEAN

Harryette Mullen is the author of **Tree Tall Woman, Trimmings**, and short stories published in the anthologies **Her Work, South by Southwest,** and **Common Bonds**. Born in the same Alabama town as W.C. Handy, she grew up in Texas, and currently lives in Ithaca, New York, a stop on the old Underground Railroad. She used to shop at Buddies and Piggly Wiggly. Now she gets her groceries at Oasis and Green Star.

SINGING HORSE PRESS TITLES

Ammiel Alcalay, *the cairo notebooks*. 1993, $9.50.

Asa Benveniste, *Invisible Ink*. Co-published with Branch Redd Books. 1989, $4.00.

Charles Bernstein, *Artifice of Absorption*. 1987, $5.00.

Julia Blumenreich, *Meeting Tessie*. 1994, $6.00.

Rachel Blau DuPlessis, *Draft X: Letters*. 1990, $6.00.

Robert Fitterman, *Among the Cynics*. 1989, OP.

Karen Kelley, *Her Angel*. 1992, $7.50.

Kevin Killian and Leslie Scalapino, *Stone Marmalade*. 1996, $9.50.

Kush, *The End Befallen Edgar Allen Poe—1849*. 1982, $2.00.

David Miller, *Unity*. 1981, $3.00.

Harryette Mullen, *Muse & Drudge*. 1995, $12.50.

Harryette Mullen, *S*PeRM**K*T*. 1992, $8.00.

Gil Ott, *Traffic (Books I & II)*. 1985, $2.50.

Ted Pearson, *Soundings*. 1980, OP.

Rosmarie Waldrop, *Differences for Four Hands*. 1984, OP.

Craig Watson, *Drawing A Blank*. 1980, OP.

Vassilis Zambaras, *Aural*. 1984, $2.00.